World as Mystery
(2016)

*

essay

*

Traumear

Paperback ISBN 978-0-244-52597-2

*

www.traumear.com

World as Mystery

The *delightful* side of mystery is the one that has both attracted and impressed me from the time of my childhood. Indeed during my childhood – and a prolonged one it was, though perhaps somewhat thinly spread, unavoidably so in the face of the afflicted state of the poor world at the time – during the years of my childhood that mystery was all I knew. Indeed it affected me favourably, as I recall now, whether from above or from below, from within or from without.

I very much doubt that such quantities as we mean by conscious intention and reflection have bearing on what we are as children. So when I mention the *delightful* side or aspect of what both seems and truly is mysterious, I mean to imply a quantity of meaning. It is my belief, for but one instance, that childhood, for those who have happened to mislay it, may be regained. More, it may be reinstated in its rightful place, by the adult who, under the burden of moral confusion and devotion to any of a variety of forever available golden calves, has repressed or merely – innocently enough, perhaps – mislaid it as of no profitable account.

What if there were nothing else to happiness beyond the recapture of our forsaken childhood? Would that not amount to much? Perhaps it should be reminded that the various so-called stages of our life are not to be passed through as painlessly as possible and left behind but that each, from the earliest to the latest, is to contribute to the degree and abundance of our life as we grow. In whatever way we prefer to imagine this growth, whether from wide-eyed simplicity to pregnant complexity or as our resurrection out of one-dimensional obtuseness to multidimensional wisdom; indeed whether we like to imagine ourselves as reborn into communal responsiveness or educated and

1

trained to the disciplines of creative maturity; we will not wish to dismiss permanently out of hand either what has been gained during childhood, youth, early manhood or womanhood etc, or what we might have gained but ignored and may now catch up.

Mystery, as substantial, lends itself readily to any and all of this. Let us understand it therefore not as a confusion that ought to be 'cleared up' in the interest of logic or as a romantic sentiment to be banished by rationality but indeed as the oil without which all else that is valid must grind to a halt.

*

The distinct possibility exists of a mystery that may be fashioned. I mean the benign mystification all but required to keep at arm's length those who much prefer to grind along in what they call their life. From personal experience we have it to a profusion quite in excess of the readily bearable, that they delight in criticism for the sake of it. To be precise, they delight in it because it confirms them in their obtuseness. We have – I should say that I have – no wish to challenge them in their stance or over the tack they take. Their delight is not the one I mean when I speak of delight as an aspect of mystery.

The sole purpose of this fashioned mystery is the eventual communication in peace with those who as yet have not found any use for mystery and perhaps they suppose they cannot abide it because they feel obliged to consider that it leads to no material advantage, while in fact what mystery does do is make material advantage itself properly manageable.

Salt makes palatable – oil makes manageable.

We do well to train ourselves in the appreciation of mystery. This may have to be mentioned now and again, because we like to deduce one thing from another and each from the previous. Understandably then, all we can say 'about' mystery, in addition to our demonstration of this quantity, must somehow remain mysterious.

It is, then, especially during moments and periods of renewal, that mystery comes into its own, inasmuch as it introduces itself and allows us to depend on it. Logic and rationality do not step aside so as to make room for something superior or preferable but we ourselves step back, both to reconsider and to prepare. Substantial mystery serves to that end.

* *

Eventually we come to see that 'world' is mysterious; not the world, that mythic entity, but real world, endless world, and it affects us mysteriously. Its effect on us is sacramental, we know that by now, because we have come to see it and to process it.

Then why do we often – some do it all their lives – go to such lengths to make certain of the finite world when we at least suspect that meanwhile we are strung out on a fool's errand? It all makes sense when we look at the world and at our often consuming attempts to make certain of it – to explain it, in other words – from the point of view of world.

Every child has initial experience of world. Either the mystery does not put the child off or it knows how to cope and therefore is not mystified. As the child is taken in hand by adults who very much mind the uncertainty of the experience from world and who take pains to manufacture artificial certainty at the expense and to the exclusion of mystery, that child is gradually accommodated to the world, the world that ends, the myth. Very sad this is, when we think of all that has to be killed off in that child.

So world is mysterious.

What needs to be answered now is why we are so reluctant to learn how to deal with world and to sustain, to benefit from, the mystery it generates in us human beings.

*

3

What I mean by world is not a state, like the world, but it induces growth, maturation and fruitfulness. All being is world-being. That means that all beings develop, while human beings also evolve.

Growth is world-induced. All beings other than human beings thrive on account of this inducement. Human beings have problems because they tend to have a will of their own. Human will and intellect can get in the way of this world-inducement. All the same, will and intellect are important for evolution. So something additional is required if human beings are to be world-capable, otherwise the evolutionary tendency innate in us tends to backfire and instead of thriving, human beings deteriorate, in the great number of ways with which we are all too familiar.

The additional element that makes us human beings as complete as all other beings, which do not evolve, is faith and suffering. We are, of course, at liberty to reject suffering and to have little faith, and to insist on our will and intellect, both at the expense of world-mystery, and therefore of world and growth. While we actually insist on our will and intellect, world-mystery appears to prevent us and seems to get in the way. This apparent prevention unfortunately then occurs to us as confusion which, we suppose, needs to be cleared up. The seeming obstruction mystifies us and we long for explanations. What we imagine as clarity is always will- and intellect-clarity and the explanations that will satisfy us will have to satisfy our will and intellect.

When we learn to suffer – which is not the same as being in pain but quite the opposite – the apparent obstruction due to insistence on will and intellect is removed, or does not occur in the first place, and when we learn to have faith – which is not little faith – world-mystery no longer seems to get in our way but instead facilitates our progress and eases growth.

*

I say that world mystery appears to get in our way while we insist on will and intellect but of course it is our *insistence* on will and intellect that gets in the way of world mystery and causes the confusion which we then strive to clear up with increased insistence on will and intellect. We can narrow this down a bit by saying that any use of will and intellect in the absence of faith and suffering causes us to experience confusion. If now we actually insist on will and intellect, expecting such behaviour to clear the confusion, we in fact cause obstructions to occur. In a funny way we can compare this to such times as when we speak heartlessly to someone. When we notice the consternation we cause, we take this for culpable obstruction and we shout. This is quite a common type of child-abuse, especially in some schools and families, though we do not refer to it by the name it deserves.

Our development tends to begin – and can be arrested – during childhood. Our evolution becomes possible – and can be avoided – during adulthood.

During our childhood and our youth we need to be raised. Any mature adults in our community can help us to come to terms – as we grow up – with *will* and *intellect* and also with *faith* and *suffering*. Any neglect or exaggeration in any department at all causes problems and pain.

All four: intellect, will, faith and suffering, need to be developed. We say that we ourselves develop as we become increasingly familiar with what is required of us: in terms of good will rather than arrogant or weak will; of sound intellect rather than morbidity or criticism; of fundamental faith rather than gullibility or dogmatism and with cheerful, intelligent suffering rather than sacrifice or martyrdom.

We are in pursuit of knowledge here, knowledge from the hard fought for point of view of world, not of the world, so we should not be surprised if we come up with a wide spread of very specific instances. A lot of what we had, up till now, gained from the left against a bad right or from the right against a not so good left, we come up against at once now and we *behold* it.

So nothing stands in the way of our at least risking, at the present intensity of insight, the statement that while light is seen – mystery is beheld.

And what is more – a fair amount more – is the following: Once we have once or twice beheld mystery, we are distinctly beholden to it. We are, as it were, eager to do our best for it – and primarily our best for those who as yet have no notion of it and either limp to the left or race to the right – or vice versa.

I mentioned oil a short while back. Shall I also mention the anointed one? It may not suit us to recall that particular tradition, so I hesitate.

*

It would seem we humans can go as far wrong on the faith and suffering side, at the expense of will and intellect (as witness some Eastern folk) as we can miss out on faith and suffering because we put all our money – here in the West – on will and intellect, to the point, so often, of misery-making insistence on them.

Might we compare, for one instance, the insistence on will and intellect to a trivialisation of faith and suffering?

This sort of inquiry really leaves everything to be said because one attempts to behold all, the entire mystery of world at any given moment, plus whatever fades before it, which can but display its feeble side and its tragic dimension.

*

So for example, starting with suffering, as in "suffer the children to come onto me", it means not merely to put up with what bothers us, perhaps while letting people know that we want to be pitied. Once we know that problems and pains are valuable life-signals, to let us know that we are obstructing good fortune and growth and either need to change our ways or else come up with an entirely new one, will we now hate the messenger, complain about him, carry on as we were? "Your house is on fire. Quick, get out!" "Oh you are such a nuisance to tell met that! Can you not see I am trying to enjoy this movie?"

Problems and pains as fortuitous signals begin to make sense once we realize the growth principle in ourselves, which amounts to constant change in the right direction for us. We are all to develop. Some even evolve. Even while we develop we are smart to familiarize ourselves with what we can do to expedite matters and to stop ourselves from interfering. Christians might like to think of it as their resurrection from the dead, which is to say from among those who have 'nothing to fear' from life- signals because their problems and pains are dead ends, like curses. When the dead say they suffer, what they mean is that they are in pain. When they solve problems they make no actual headway. Moral and religious human beings sooner or later come out from among the dead and think intelligently, until they are able to recognize, and then to realize, the growth principle within themselves. A new life begins for them then. Their grievances no longer get them down because they develop insights into why they exist and how they can optimize their live being and their well doing.

Whether our growth is mainly moral, religious or spiritual, we do well to make good and positive sense of suffering as the eventually cheerful acceptance and understanding of whatever bothers us at any given time as both a wake-up call and as the carrier of information on what our particular contribution is to be to the realization of our growth-development. We are best placed ourselves to understand that information correctly and we will eventually learn that we never learn so well as when we confer and communicate with others who have life. Naturally communication with the dead is a non-starter.

It sounds slightly absurd that we might accept problems and pains cheerfully. Of course we flinch. Also the unpleasantness of the reminder is in direct proportion to how far we have strayed or to how much additional or new life is to come our way. Naturally the two are the same. Those who are in the know will gladly agree that the joy is greater when we mend our more serious fault.

Behold, our sins are forgiven and our misdemeanours are little ones. Even in the most moral and religious sense, our mistakes are all functions of growth during development. Forget the so-called 'holy man' who has neither problems nor pains because he neither sins nor errs. Ten to one he is dead, so have no truck with him, that is my advice. Also be not afraid of the monsters who kill and destroy, in high or low places. They don't have a clue. When their time is up they disappear in a puff of good news.

*

A few words about how best to *behold* an affliction, once we have got over the automatic reaction, which is usually hateful and fearful. Our suffering is to be intelligent, meaning that our approach to it ('approach' already suggests a useful distance) is to be as to a teaching. We are to find out how we can improve our attitude to life, our behaviour in our environment, our response to creative urges within us. Any and all of this we can learn as we behold what we experience, or know, or assume – to be our affliction.

Now we know we are immortal but it is not our ambition to be forever visible. World is not a thing; things plague us. We suffer them intelligently. We suffer the world, which is all too visible. World beheld simply is. We do well to pay a little extra attention to how we speak, to what words we use. World affects us most nobly. We know we are affected by world and it pleases us. All our growth impulses are world oriented. If by world I mean kingdom of heaven on earth, what is that to you who are wedded to the world? There is no more difference between what I realize and what is realized for me. If you cannot yet stomach the mystery of world-arrival, look forward to it and know its arrival depends on you, on your meek and mild acceptance of the message from the messenger whom you do not continue to shun.

So the message is mysterious, granted, but that is why we do not try to interpret it or to analyze it but we behold it, in the sense that we allow it to affect our whole being and our personal human nature as one. That is what it means to behold. That is our world-approach. Implied is our complete and utter trust that the remedial move for which we are responsible will be revealed to us and that the revelation will be the making of that move.

Have we not experienced all too often that as soon as we seem to ourselves to have calculated some cause for our affliction and we set about to remove it, we invariably end up – how strange and aggravating! indeed, how mysterious! – doing the exact opposite? I am depressed because I smoke too much. I shall stop smoking. I find myself smoking twice as many cigarettes. I talk too much and speak without prior reflection, I force myself to think before I open my mouth. So after a pause I blab out complete nonsense.

So the revelation is in fact the remedy. Behold, I will set you free, says the spirit of healing.

We will not succeed in adapting to world and to world-environment by instituting anything, whether we intend change or a brake on change, in the world.

The christian (sic)[1] knows that intelligent suffering unites him with the salvific spirit that is Jesus within him.

---

[1] As in my book: 'christianity'.

9

The philosopher, who makes it his task to know, knows that when he beholds his afflictions he makes it possible for the remedy to be revealed to him.

The scientist understands that not only his own but also the afflictions of others are his business, but does he accept the responsibility?

The artist (not the art-worker) tries to accept the responsibility for the ailments of his society but fails because he knows nothing of world-reality.

The art-worker frees himself of the world and creates examples of transition to world.

So we do well to think where we go for help. The philosopher, the scientist, the artist – these are generations of world-institution and afflictions in themselves that are revealed to us in modern guise so that we may be spurred on to responsible humanity in reality.

*

Next I want to make a suggestion that has direct bearing, still, on the topic of intelligent suffering and the perception I have called beholding. It is this: While we suffer and behold we are in the true *frame of being* that allows us to make sensible requests. What we ask for, in that frame of being, is not stupidly or unwisely asked. Also the response is immediate. What we request is given while we request. What we demand comes about as we demand. All depends on that true frame of being in which we know that we cannot ask or request what we do not even then possess and that we cannot demand what is not the case at that very moment, albeit hidden from us.

Once again we find ourselves in the very presence of world-mystery. I do not have to mention god because all that I describe is godly. World-mystery in the absence of the divine is unthinkable and unimaginable – as we can imagine.

*

The fact that we are now and again beset by pain and involved in problems is not to dissuade us from the teaching that even the worst imaginable catastrophe is after all at bottom a restoration of equilibrium from which we can learn how better to conduct ourselves in the future. The fact that we can no more predict the future than change the past in any real sense only confirms us in our ambition not to live in the present but in the here and now, where mystery informs us at every turn – which we find delightful, because we are never lost for an interesting slant on the increasing life that accompanies our constant growth.

Related to this we come up against the two dangers of supposing that human-natural growth is bound to be eternally steady and never abrupt, and of assuming that while we are visible on the earth we are liable to arrive at an end beyond which development and evolution are either impossible or unnecessary. We can see how the greatest danger might be described as an eclipse of the two, that is to say, of the one by the other. So for example we grow tired and interpret our tiredness as the final arrival at an end, instead of once again making ready for what this phenomenon signals, such as, for one example, a need for extra attention paid within. Or we have had such a pleasant time of it for so long that we mistake this for the status quo at the expense of even ordinary vigilance – and after a time it will take a crash of sorts to alert us.

Even the ancient wisdom speaks of our ability to ride the storm and of our willingness to surpass ourselves. All we need to add to that then, in order to rid ourselves of modern prejudices by which we self-consciously seek to dilute the truth, is the mystery of the life of faith and reason in our sacramentally impressive world-environment.

*

It may mislead to speak of constant growth. Even outwardly we are, after all, forever challenged by impressions to

11

which we want to be able to respond as wisely and cleverly as possible. We want to be able to rely on that process of incoming information and outgoing creativity for which we ourselves are responsible in that we 'keep the works well oiled' in terms of our ready appreciation of the delightful mystery that helps to define our existence on earth.

World is still nebulous to most of even those who are aware of it. Nebulous does not mean mysterious. Still, it is better than ignorance. The fact that world is impressive needs to be confined to our body of knowledge; only thereafter will we be truly impressed. Even the initial impressions of world are mysterious and we welcome them to the extent of our preparedness for being moved out and beyond our present mind-set or body-pattern. Supreme vigilance gathers the mysterious impressions into itself and presents them to us as communicable language. I realize that normally we think of language as the means of communication but in this case of world-impressions it is language itself that is being presented to us so that we might pass it on as teachings. I use the word language in the widest sense, as communication of any sort that links and bonds beings.

We are impressed by world and we collaborate in the building of world, in the erection and construction of it, along lines of any quick and easy establishment. Certainly play is not excluded. Mystery does lend itself to any sense of play in the direction of world-empowerment.

Whatever access we have to world is what we begin with. Alone our good habit of suffering rather than resisting makes us eligible. Add to that our ability to behold, especially over a period of time, and we are well on our way to being able to sustain the sort of world impressions that advance our progress without hindrance, as we sharpen our tools and activate our faculties.

How can I possibly be more specific? The wish to be led by the hand has to be buried in the soil of personal faith and authentic responsibility. Behold, you are capable of standing on your own two feet. What I am advocating in this little book is that we put an end to our individual helplessness. The fact that we cannot manipulate the world itself has possibly come home to us on the back of failure upon failure. How fortunate we are on account of those failures makes good and pleasant sense to us as soon as we stop resisting evil and instead open ourselves to world-revelation. Suddenly intrinsically successful moves are suggested to us left and right.

*

World *revelation*, all still due to suffering and beholding, is one side of the coin. World *creation* is the other.

We mustn't allow ourselves to pretend, when we speak of world-creation, that what we create is world itself. That after all has been done, and for us. What we create is what makes world visible, which is to say sensible, tangible. And that, of course, has to mean sensible, tangible, for a few, for several and for many. That would describe part of our work. We can certainly do with a bit of a description because when it comes to these mysterious impressions and touches, especially at first, it seems hard indeed not to be able to get into the thick of it – especially if one seems to need that – which, of course, no one does.

So, on the creative rather than the revealed side now, we do not halt at impressionism. We do as much as we can and then a bit extra. We know we are on to a good thing, we no longer have to be told that, even though downhill from every phenomenon that comes our way a bog persuades uphill progress. We behold a mysterious object and supply the subject. We observe a mysterious move and supply one of our own, to keep it company. We can go as far as we like from the point of view of our creative bias and we know that those who choose to draw benefit from our work have the world-mystery revealed to them. If, however, they have what it takes to begin with re-

13

vealed world, they will very likely – no, quite for sure, actually – let it be known what they see and touch. Visions, sights and contacts can all abound for us, when it comes to that. The realization of the kingdom of god on earth is a many-splendoured affair. Those who participate are those who benefit and those who benefit will participate.

*

It would not occur to us to suffer in the way described here if we did not have faith. Without faith it makes no sense to suffer because all we can think of in that case is the avoidance of all that is unpleasant and inconvenient. Faith make possible the spiritual perspective that allows us to view world four-dimensionally. Time no longer holds any terror for us, so we make no effort to hide from ourselves the incessant passage of hours, days and years. As a consequence time becomes mysterious in itself. We no longer hurry but are glad to wait for the time for this or that to ripen, even though the least diminishment of faith would right away make us fear for our survival.

The difference between little faith and fundamental faith is highlighted when we realize that fundamental faith cannot work – and all true faith is working faith – unless we are able to sustain to at least some degree the mystery of time. For the materialist time is nothing more than what can be calculated, with the help of clocks and calendars. For the spiritualist it does not even exist. The mystery of it becomes relevant in our lives as soon as we begin to experience eternal time, which is mysterious throughout.

Faith makes possible our experience of both eternal time and eternal life because it allows us to sustain the mystery of these, which attracts us.

*

So world commences to interest us as substantial mystery, that is to say as mystery we suffer and behold. Why do we not reject this mystery in favour of objective certainty, which de-

stroys life, or on the basis of subjective conviction, which ig-
nores life? Simply for the reason that we have experience, even
historical awareness, of such destruction and ignoration and
because we have faith, which makes it practicable for us to sustain this world-mystery as substantially lively – and live.

We notice the role reason plays here. I think of reason as
my life-support system. It informs me of the intrinsic intercon-
nection of world and life – of world without end and eternal
life. It reminds me, if ever I forget, of the appreciable importance of faith and suffering and it keeps me right in terms of
faith as not enthusiastic-gullible but fundamental and of what it
means to suffer, not painfully but intelligently and cheerfully.

So reason is the valued, the indispensible, companion, the
helpmeet, and I sacrifice nothing but gain a great deal if I keep
that companion by me. Sometimes I think of faith and reason
as the flesh and blood of enlightened thought, but that is only
to prevent me from sliding into any number of modern absurdi-
ties that pit faith and reason against each other, meaning, of
course, little faith and critical reason, i.e. criticism.

World as mystery therefore is logically the beginning of
world for us and not to be superseded. The fact that world-
revelation is initially mysterious does not imply that as we become more world-familiar the mystery passes. We always require this important aspect of world if we are to live and not
merely to exist, because world-mystery is delightful and delight allows us initially to step out of survival-priority into life-
prosperity.

*

I want to limit myself in this book to world both initially
and thereafter as mysterious. I consider this to be a serious
enough undertaking. If we are ever to evolve out of our merely
developmental notion of world as 'the world', in other words
as not real but mythic, we have to overcome a few hindrances
to our progress, such as the suspicious fear that the world is not

15

really life-sustaining (which it is not) and that life as nothing but materialistic survival is all that is possible for us in such a world, (which is correct). When we begin even to contemplate eternal life, which we intrinsically feel to be our true heritage, we soon despair of ever being able to live such a life in a world that is rent irreparably by internal contradictions.

What we need to believe in therefore is the world-mystery that is revealed to us as we behold it. The revelation and the beholding are one and the same just as the believing and the substantiality of it are one and the same. Certainly we can contemplate each in distinction; as the two sides of the one coin, however, and not as a separate unique entities.

We behold the mystery and we believe what we behold. That is to say, we do not subject what we behold to any preliminary critique in order to separate out what is not worth believing and accepting. That again would be treating world as a developmental entity and as something that can be interpreted or changed. It is *the world* that languishes in contradictions, such as capitalism versus socialism, contradictions that are intensified until they become 'global', which signals the highest possible degree of world-emergency. As world emerges, due to the work of those who understand and testify to it and equally due to the fact that the time for it is ripe, the merely developmental, mythic world, which seems to need to be interpreted and changed but can never be made really life-supportive, gradually appears to withdraw into itself, the way a flower naturally wilts when the fruit is ready to form.

Human-natural evolution begins suddenly in those – and is begun by those – who have what it takes to sustain it and to testify to it – nothing much more can really be said about that particular aspect of the transformation; which is also a transubstantiation; however not in the sense that one substance is changed into another but rather in that the thing that was assumed to be substantial but in reality was not, is superseded by real and fundamental substance.

*

Here we finally arrive at a notion of what it properly means 'to believe in', rather than just to believe. We say we 'believe in' the world-mystery we behold as revealed. What we 'believe in' is necessarily not objective or subjective but it embraces us and we embrace it. In other words, it affords us rest. For once we can even playfully relax in our pursuits of what is important – to us and for us, and therefore also for others. We advance in leisurely fashion, sure of ourselves, in no need of approval or applause. Such marvellous assurance as comes over us we could in nowise have achieved, neither by improving ourselves nor by altering our circumstances. We can readily settle into this rest without in any way compromising our vigilance or our agility. You might say that we come into the possession of our true stature.

What with this 'inbelief', the mystery 'thickens'. That is to say, world-mystery is no longer merely a confrontational phenomenon but now any one of an infinite number of opportunities for exercise, by which I mean restful coming out of ourselves and merging with world, mostly in terms of behaviour.

It would be wrong that prior to this we were somehow trapped or enclosed within ourselves, whatever that might mean. No, what I am delineating here has nothing to do with realistic life-progression. We do not walk around for a while gaping at the mystery that is world before we take the next step towards something like full world-involvement. What concerns me is rather a case of gradually coming to a thorough understanding of something that happens suddenly, in the blink of an eye, as someone has called it, or as during a flash of lightning. Thereafter one sets out to come to terms with it. So technically what I am giving you, the reader, is one of a great variety of possible versions of how I myself have come to terms with it. I

17

am delineating my evolution, not describing my development, or someone else's development. Or development in general. Development is gradual, over a period of time but evolution is sudden, in the sense of a total change and no common denominator exists between before and after. Even memory is changed –plus of course our entire sense apparatus and the way we perceive ourselves.

The greatest difficulty of course always arises for those who are in nowise prepared for their evolution. What they experience is merely the diminishment of their developmental faculties and functions, while that which is completely new finds no welcome within them. What happens then is that those who participate in their evolution, making sense of it and coming to terms with it, try their best to co-exist with those who might have evolved but failed to do so and can best be described as being stuck in a non-developmental cul-de-sac, with whom true communication is impossible. We come across examples and types of evolution in all beings and to our own eyes what we 'behold' is always something like an external uniformity and an internal complexity which remains mysterious – unless we poke around in it and probably destroy it.

The most typical example of evolution is the seed, that contains the potentiality of some specimen. No common denominator exists that allows us honestly and with integrity to link what comes afterwards with what exists before – before the breaking out of the shell of that which can only suppositionally be said to have developed inside the shell. The fact that favourable conditions are required for an egg to 'hatch', for a seed to sprout, or whatever technical terms are used in these various examples of development to evolution, should not be overlooked. Also, fertilization and hatching are to be viewed distinctly, whether we concentrate on the natural life of people, of animals or plants and so on. The fertilization amounts to an introduction of something entirely new, while the hatching implies favourable conditioning.

So we can say that the fertilized egg evolves once it is hatched. The sudden change is called birth, unless we want to make up some other word for it.[2] The popular idea of 'birth, copulation and death' describes nothing but <u>mere</u> development, which is to say development not towards the possibility of evolution. It is what we then sadly describe as the process of survival. As human beings we can do better than merely to survive until death obliterates us. A description of how we get on that is more suitable than 'birth, copulation and death' would therefore be development and evolution.

So development and evolution instead of 'birth, copulation and death'. We can become so involved, to our detriment, in the birth-copulation-death paradigm that we lose all perspective until all things are one thing and everything is nothing. So we have to be very decisive about what we choose to look at and what we choose to ignore. Not all and everything that can be looked at is worth looking at.

So, for example, when I say that world reveals itself mysteriously, I right away do well to add that what we so wonderfully gain due to that revelation can, in fact, not be gained by 'looking at'. If we now suppose that since 'looking at' seems to imply objectivity, we must evidently now take to the subjective, we soon discover that lo and behold, our imagination goes wild, as I indicated a few paragraphs ago.

'Beholding', therefore, must be our evolutionary tactic. If we have been 'fertilized' by merciful good spirit and if we are

---

[2] A discussion of how there is no common denominator between the seed and the plant, between the embryo and the born being, would take us too far at this point. Worth repeating, however, that our human nature, as we were born, carries the secret of world as mystery. Subsequent development implies the possibility of going astray and the need for favourable circumstances.

persuaded that indeed this divine and unconditional love has considered us worthy of attention, then we will feel obliged to step out of that birth-copulation-death syndrome as we espouse our ongoing evolution.

No need in either case to break our heads over problems of relativity. All we need to decide is: Are we spiritual beings or not. Usually we do not agonize for very long over whether we want to be concert pianists or not; over whether we intend to stake all on becoming religious leaders or moral teachers. Mostly our vanity is to blame, when we confuse special selection with prestige, and that is how one causes oneself difficulties. Even the successful concert pianist or violinist knows that if he is to benefit personally and in reality from being 'the first' (in terms of development) among those who are similarly selected by birth and training, he does well to strive to be the least among them (on the basis of evolution), otherwise he invites complications.

So while this profound wisdom of deciding to be the least if one wants to be the first applies to talent, how much more does it apply to the status of human being, when not only some part of us turns out to be exceptional but we ourselves are exceptional, perhaps even as spiritual human beings – and therefore joyfully burdened with the greatest responsibility of all!

*

The concepts of faith and suffering have served us as we acquainted ourselves initially with world as mystery, revealed to us as substantial and believable. In addition I mentioned will and intellect, that will allow us to add to this delightful aspect of world. Let no one assume that I am devising a philosophic system of the old style, that would amount to an attempt to say the last word about something. I merely say what I see here and now, and I value most of all if others do the same. What is seen and who sees it is inseparable.

Will, then, especially as willingness, namely to be invested by world-mysterious substance, is always a meek and mild type of constitution, or even institution, of ourselves. To be willing in a certain way, in this case, means to bring forward all our faculties for ready cooperation with world-effect. The fact that we truly live implies after all that we do not reject but accept the effect – the manifold and various effects and affects – of world-mystery. Any willingness to cooperate with how we find ourselves, inarguably due to being in world, works in our favour. Further explanation of this willingness we arrive at by realizing that in the absence of it we suppose we are exposed and that circumstances impose themselves upon us. The willingness I am advocating therefore is positive in the best sense of the word. In the train of it we often experience a surge of clarity and above all vitality and freedom. The freedom is not the liberty due to lack of responsibility but it implies increased ability to respond to what- or whoever might benefit from our response. Whether benign or benevolent, our willingness links us in lively fashion into various suitable world processes which become habitual for us.

We can see how world is increasingly revealed to us as good habit. We are to be at home on earth and this is to come true for us. World means good habit instead of trial, testing, affliction and agony. So I speak of our willingness rather than of the will, which is mythic again and forever developmental, which is to say merely developmental, like an attempt to get a flower to bloom forever and supposing that preventing any fruit from evolving will do the trick.

What we study, we momentarily separate and divide. Our willingness is in truth not a faculty as such, not a tool but one of our many functions. It is ourselves both reaching out for world and being world-informed. In other words we recognize world in ourselves within us, as equal to world outwardly approachable. So we extend ourselves willingly even while world

21

affection (or world-affect) intends us at times and we recognize the difference. The will as such is therefore pointless. We may be willing or unwilling but so may world-actuality.

Not a bad time to speak of world-actuality because thank god it varies so much from one of us to the next. World-actuality and world-factuality correspond, then, to our willingness to be moved and to be touched. We can see how crucial it must be for us to divest ourselves of as much bigotry and of as many prejudices as possible. Alas, it is by being willing, not by self-criticism, that we rid ourselves of these. Not by engaging with what is false and bad do we remove our penchant to it in ourselves but by exercising and entertaining a willingness to be touched and moved by world.

Not only is world good, but it is dependably whole. One might say that its primal effect on adults is to cause them to ask themselves, are they whole. World-substance as sacramental is familiar to us by now. It should not surprise us that we feel inclined to call that which is whole holy. It is wholely (sic). Its being, after all, is that of god. World is of god. What could be more convenient for us human beings who seek to be at home on earth without having to worry about our survival; which is, so to speak, god's responsibility! Divine spirit forever and always creates world for us so that we might survive. This cannot in any way make real sense to us unless we at least desire to live and to have life. While we are merely ambitious to survive, we take god's work out of god's hands, as it were, and world then is bound to occur to us as mythic, as the world, this world, the bad old world – depending on our mental categories. All of this lies outside our present frame of reference, of course and I only mention it to create perspective. Moral man certainly continues to do his work in full recognition of the fact that what he does well contributes to his wellbeing and what he depends on most to allow him to be himself in the right is the rightness of universal law. Religious man, by comparison, is grateful for his natural environment and does his work as a thanksgiving, in contribution to the welfare of all and in cooperation with his god. Religious man is of course also moral. Spiritual man, who is also religious and moral, works to do good on behalf of all and makes no distinction between life and survival. His main work contribution, in terms of this present essay, is to identify world in a variety of ways for those who are inept in the world because they have been touched or moved sacramentally.

It makes no sense to world-related human beings to speak of 'free will' in the sense of someone being at liberty to will whatever he likes because such human beings, as we have indicated, do not 'will' anything in the first place. They do not possess a will, nor an intellect, as I intend to show shortly. Such a will is an idea and one is liable to be possessed by such an idea to the extent that one remains connected to the world and especially if one prefers to be bound by it. A religious man might speak of the world as underwritten by angels in whose interest it remains to keep human beings dependent upon them, and this then explains, again for a religious person, the eternal struggle between good and bad in the world, since there are good angels and bad angels, all of whom resent the fact that God prefers humans to angels. If this works for someone as an explanation of the world as something to be traded in for world-sacrament, then surely it serves a good purpose.

The world itself can of course be seen and even 'experienced' as an idea but as we well know, ideas can never be fully realized. World, by comparison, is fully realized and requires no effort from us to make it acceptable. Spontaneous action, habitual behaviour and intentional being and doing merely require a general or a specific willingness for world-relation and we will automatically opt for one or the other – I mean for specific or general willingness, depending on whether we want to be effective or affective, which is to say whether we want to bring something about or actually bring it into existence in the first place. Rally we do not have to think about this at all. It suffices that we know how at times our willingness seems to have a different character.

All of our juggling with will and intellect as though they were faculties with which we need to conjure to achieve certain admirable ends, is therefore productive of greater attachment to the world, no matter how enthusiastically or dogmatically we argue for freedom of the will and sharpness of the intellect, and for all that may be attained through them, not excluding the greatest wonders of civilization and marvels of technology. Equally all our resistance of evil, whether we return an insult or throw hydrogen bombs at each other, is willed ideality that can only be stopped if we choose meek and mild world-willingness instead; meek and mild, and perfectly reasonable.

World as whole and therefore sacramentally productive of wholeness in all beings that relate to it is easy enough to imagine because we come equipped with our endowed human nature within us – as our within-realm. However world as good cannot make sense to us unless we actually, physically and truthfully, prefer what is good, otherwise that aspect of world must irritate, inconvenience and confuse us, so that as a consequence we busy ourselves with this then and sacrifice true world-relation.

From within ourselves we learn to want what is good and we develop a preference for it, for moral, religious or spiritual good. We yearn for it and we desire it from within and now world can reveal itself to us as ethically predetermined, and as our world-relation is sanctified, which means that it can no longer be interrupted.

Some are bound to say: Whatever our desire for what is good, we still have to live in the world as it is, namely a mixture of bad and good, so is there any point in holding out this ideal of world that is good and whole? We cannot close our eyes to the evil in the world, nor should we want to. Our only hope is to change the world, to make it good.

Others will say: Evidently what you mean by world has to be created by us, so that gradually it will replace what you mean by the world. Therefore we ourselves first have to be good and only then can we bring about this revolution – which has, of course, been tried innumerable times but always those who make the effort are themselves not up to it in the end.

I intend to respond to both of these arguments at once. On one hand we have to realize that we cannot be good. We can do good but we cannot be good. On the other hand, world is not an ideal. As for the argument that we have to live in the world, this stems from the modern supposition that life and the world are separate entities and that we can live in the world without being part of it. This is a comforting illusion, nothing more. Those cling to it who think of themselves as good. They steer clear of the more rapacious worldliness, which is perhaps easy enough for them because they have neither talent nor drive. Any predatory motivations they keep well hidden, even from themselves, by means of all sorts of psychic tricks and supernatural diversion. None of that is a step in the direction of world.

Also let us remind ourselves again of the good news that the world is not real but an ideal and therefore more or less mighty. It is as mighty as we make it and as mighty a we allow it to become for us. The might of it derives from the fact that it presents itself to us as something that might be realizable. Unless we have a notion of that which can in truth and fact be realized, namely world as substantial mystery rather than the world as any number of fugitive ideas and ideals and utopias, we are liable to accept one promissory note after the other, none of which will ever be honoured. Happy those who find this out early and are delighted.

No one has to live in the world. Not only do we not have to be part of the world but we do not have to live in it. Actually, no one really does live in the world. We only live to the extent that we are world inhabitants. The genuine character of our communality depends on our living in world. If at the same time we suppose we need to arrive at various compromises with the world, that then is our predicament and our choice. All the same – whether altogether from the point of view of spirituality or from that of religion or even from that of morality – world as holy sacrament and as substantial mystery is available. It reveals itself, presents itself or simply is.

Why should we want to close our eyes to the evil in the world? What matters is that we do not resist it but instead set good examples, in person and through all our works. It would make better sense if we spoke instead of the evil of the world. If we came to see the falsehood inherent in every idea, and embodied in every ideal, and advertised in the name of any and all idealistic utopias, we would wish neither to close our eyes to evil nor to resist it but we would see it clearly for what it is and for all it amounts to, namely, in every instance, a more or less tragic error of judgment, attitude and behaviour. It is in the fullest awareness of the evil in and of the world that we do real good, not in hiding from it behind and within institutions, organizations and societies.

*

What, finally then, does intellect amount to when we see it in its true relation to 'world as revealed mystery'?

We do like to think of ourselves as capable of thought and we depend a lot on this ability, more or less developed through practice and application. We depend on it not only when we order our affairs but also when we strike out into new areas of knowledge and understanding. So when we have grown to the point where development becomes evolution, if and when this is on the cards for us, then we notice, for one example, how our environment is no longer questionable, encouraging us, as it were, to think and to think more magnanimously, generously and caringly, for example, but our thought is reflected on itself by that very environment, as if it were no longer now a case of ourselves getting to know and understand the environment so that we might, perhaps, teach to others what we discover, but instead we become thoughtful and enterprising. We become thoughtful for others.

The intellect itself, which often becomes something of a traditional hobby-horse in the playroom of those who insist on idealistic development as the be-all and end-all of human endeavour, this intellect is no longer allowed to insist on itself now, as the master of mentality, because our mind and our body are no longer separate but one, as a loving thoughtfulness – in relation to world as revealed mystery; or as revealing mystery, because it does, after all, also reveal much about ourselves as evolving human beings.

Whether we mean intuition, intelligence or intellect, all these have to do with teaching and learning. We teach as we learn now and we learn as we teach, on account of our world-relation. How obvious it must seem to us now that what we have observed and examined as the world is neither a realm of magic that needs to be exorcized by means of some systematic belief-system, nor is it an emergency-shelter for materialists, where everything that emerges is fodder for successive analysis and synthesis, in the hope that this will forestall human evolution, which cannot but occur as a threat to us if we have made up our mind about life being finally and merely developmental and therefore idealistically so.[3] The modern theory of evolution, as an explanation for the great variety of life-forms, is just such an attempt to divert the human gaze so that we shall not

---

[3] Mere development, necessarily idealistic, or development towards evolution.

be tempted to behold the marvellous beauty of all that lives as we support and sustain it in our official capacity as stewards of the earth. As atheistic materialists we stand in the desert and gaze at the setting sun and we say: How beautiful! We have our moment and we like to cling to it. As inhabitants of world on earth we deem ourselves fortunate to be able both to exist and to live at once, thoughtfully, gratefully and wide awake, in world without end.

*

Not only are we faced with objection to world-mystery due to our insistence on will and intellect. Equally there is the pandemic little-faith and the equation of suffering with pain to be considered as *subjection* to world-mystery.

The objections are removed to the extent that we become proficient at intelligent suffering in profound faith. This I have mentioned earlier. Now we can also see how, to the degree that we learn to be thoughtful and willing in the face of world mystery, that very subjection is now removed and we are, as a consequence, less enfeebled and no longer pessimistic about our chances for a full and rich life.

*

World mystery delights us. We also stand in awe of it.

This experience of awe is well worthy of acknowledgment. If we ignore it or give it no credence it occurs to us merely as dread and we will try to avoid it. World-mystery as awe, however, invites us to internalize imaginatively the sacramental substance, very much in the same way as we internalize any other food.

The dread we feel, the fear and panic we sense, is of world and specifically of world-mystery, not of the world. The world is what we come up with in reaction to all the worry that accumulates within us. We are fearful to the extent that we do not trust and are not courageous in response to world-mystery. All

28

the various aspects of what we mean by the world, such as society, nationality, popularity, private and public existence and
such, are apprehensive anticipations of, and defence measures
against, world-mystery which unfortunately is not known in
that case as a blessing but purposefully, even ambitiously and
energetically, ignored.

No doubt some are born who right away have within them
that essential increment of knowledge and understanding of the
sacramental beauty and truth that challenges them from without
and in a sense they rest in awe of god-created and god-sustained
world while they make it their life's task to offer to others the
meaning of world, often in spite of the resistance of those who
are committed to the cowardly rejection of sacramental values.
However they are in the minority. We who know about the difference between world and the world, between the reality and
the myth, can get together and ask in the spirit that more such
supremely gifted ones will be made available.

Courage, underpinned by informed trust, is what allows us
to overcome any ingrained distrust of that which initially
probes us and we tremble. We tremble because we are unfamil-
iar with world as such and with its whole and good essentiality.
Metaphorically one might say that the first time we stand on
holy ground we tremble – to the degree of our partiality. However do we overcome our partiality? Can we make ourselves
whole so that world will not shock us?

What we can do is courageously overcome our partial in-
clinations for the time it takes to measure up to some world-
mysterious challenge, which we recognize due to the dread that
rises in us and to which we feel inclined, in cowardly fashion,
to react by turning to the world.

*

How problematic, that for us moderns true awe is as unrec-
ognizable as true delight? How telling that when we describe
something as awful nowadays we refer to its bad quality? Do

29

we have a word to describe ourselves when we are in awe? I feel inclined to invent the word 'aweful' to refer to the state or condition of someone who is full or awe. Why not? An aweful person is a beautiful person because the glory of god is within him (her) and he (she) experiences the kingdom of god on earth, which is world; which is mysterious and sacramental.

Is it any wonder that we moderns with our split personality and our uncertain individuality, our separate body and mind, our little faith, our unwillingness to suffer intelligently and to be physically thoughtful – that we are terrified by such an actuality to the point where we are stupefied and dumbfounded?

A spiritual man will ask himself: How can I be and behave, how can I act and what can I do, so that world-mystery may become palatable to at least some of those who live in hope and refuse to be daunted. Their hope is for world to be actual and they refuse to be daunted by governments and institutions. They hope to be able to see what they feel and to think what they know and they will not be daunted by the fear of what is strange and different. In the face of world-mystery, what they find is that their entire belief-system is challenged, if they have one. Needless to say, all reactions are individual. If I am committed to a system of beliefs and assumptions, whether political or religious, I will not react to a challenge of these as you yourself would or as your best friend would. The best common denominator I can come up with is dread. We are rocked back on our heels. What is quickly revealed to us is whether we have a foundation for our human being. If we do not, we will, very likely, cower right away behind any pack of lies we can come up with on the spur of the moment, which simply means then that world is not for us just yet. We may get another chance, who can say. If, however, our human being is well founded, we will find that we come up with the courage required for countenancing world-mystery in one way or another and right away we will wish to declare ourselves in favour. We will celebrate.

Each one of us will, however, find him- or herself celebrating in a unique manner and fashion, which in turn will inspire some others with the courage for rising to the occasion of some world-challenge. Hopefully a time will come soon when we are no longer 'rocked back on our heels' in the advent of world-mystery but instead gently reminded that once again the time has come for an adjustment to an increase. Very likely we will, in the meantime, have learned how to make our own contribution to the active celebration of 'god's kingdom on earth as in heaven'.[4]

*

The role and use of imagination is important as we receive, and become receptive of, world through world mystery. A great variety of imaginative responses are, of course, possible. What is always bound to interest ourselves first is the image that suits us best. The suggestion that we form images to suit us begs the question: Who are we and what is our reason for forming images?

Two complexes of knowledge need to be drawn into consideration here. We do well to remind ourselves perhaps that our main and central interest, when it comes to world-knowledge, is human beings. How we see ourselves as human beings determines how we see all other beings. Our personal integrity dictates that we treat other beings truthfully, reasonably and justly. So I intend to take advantage of what we have learned so far of the difference between moral, religious and spiritual humanity. Beyond that I consider it to be of especial importance in the present direction of our research that we keep in mind the communal aspect of our nature – by which I mean the need to shy away from individual isolation, always prefer-

---

[4] As christians we periodically need to be reminded that the kingdom of heaven is not an ideal and futuristic state but intimate reality, which implies 'persecution'. In a way we may as readily be pursued by enemies as by a toothache.

ring to achieve our ends – in the present case, to be sure, world-knowledge as our goal – by leaning on one another and learning from one another.

A familiarity with world-mystery in terms of *morality* depends upon images that can be handled almost as if they were of practical use, such as for eating and drinking, sleeping and waking, also standing, walking, sitting and the like. All such images appeal to the moral aspect of our human nature, mainly because they refer to what can be done more or less well and in community with others. They appeal to our moral character. Those who are not particularly interested in religious relation or in the reality of religion, can achieve for themselves a reasonable world view by recognizing how all beings are capable of optimum performance and by acknowledging, beyond that, how they themselves, as moral human beings, achieve greater satisfaction and happiness by extending the fruits of their morality to other beings.

Reason, happily, is understood by all human beings and our imagination is always at least reasonable, if not creative. As a direct consequence, avarice cannot touch us. This is good news indeed, since avarice is the main enemy of communal cooperation. The self-serving approach is immoral and therefore inimical to true world-perception. An avaricious man might make up images for himself as a successful survivor which cannot hold because they cannot be referred to his human nature. Also whatever we do poorly, whether we believe and imagine poorly or engender bad quality in our work, however we dress it up to deceive ourselves, removes us from world and ties us to the world, even if only by taste and predilection.

It might be helpful to remind once again, at this stage, that human beings, unlike people, cannot be typecast. If we refer to the moral man, we do not mean anyone who can actually exist. The moral man, like the religious and the spiritual man, is an image that allows us to concentrate suggestively what we mean. If then we describe a moral man, we mean someone whose view of life and world makes most reasonable sense to him in terms of righteousness, of good and bad, of well and poor. He feels most comfortable to think in those terms. All the same he is able to think and is grateful for being in the possession of that skill. Those who are unwilling to think or have lost the ability due to lack of use, instead indulge in popularity and in guarding, not themselves but their self, first and foremost against world-mystery because quite rightly they are apprehensive of it and see it as the enemy of their self or ego. People have a false image of themselves as their self, which they cherish, nourish and defend. We do well to respect them nonetheless, because not to do so is impolite and also impolitic. In addition, something might even be said in favour of a small degree of popularity because it provides what we can think of as a negative frame for any world-image to which we intend to resort creatively. Genius is most aware of this during the course of elemental creativity.

*

One of the major difficulties for just about anyone nowadays is presented by virtual reality because of how it affects our imagination. Generally, while we are still attached to the world, we imagine what we like and accept that as valid currency until circumstances force us to imagine otherwise. In an important sense however this does violence to a capacity we have from birth as an aspect of unconditional love. While our love is practically unconditional, during infancy in any case, our imagination does not operate as a separate entity. Gradually then, as we become modernized and are taught the ways of the world – actually taught them, as is all too often the case – imagination becomes one thing and love another. Images and pictures, like pain and suffering, become interchangeable while unconditional, imagination-rich love goes out the window and is seen from afar by well-meaning individuals as an ideal. In other words, this divine love, which all human beings would wish to be able to practice and actuate, is no longer viable because a defensive bulwark of this-worldliness has been erected, which keeps imagination infertile and separate from love – that is selfish.

While art, as we moderns have long understood it, is tasked with making us feel alright with being attached to the world, even consoling us for it and making us momentarily forget our predicament, supra-modern virtual reality, as we are coming to know it, combines selfish love with infertile imagination in a single extinct package, so that by buying into it we are no longer bothered by the discrepancy between selfish love and infertile imagination. This discrepancy had at least kept us informed of this aspect of our tragic modern state and had alerted us now and then, uncomfortably of course, to the human need for unconditional love. Virtual reality 'experience' blots out the misfortune and the discomfort and replaces a psychic dilemma with a psychosis, that varies somewhat from individual to individual, however only until complete brain-death sets in. Thereafter all are one and the same – and dispensable.

For the one who seeks to furnish himself with true world-knowledge, resistance of evil is out of the question. Virtual reality, even as it amounts to a comparative comfort from the world's point of view, from the point of view of world it is an evil. So that is where the difficulty for all human beings sets in. One recognizes and feels the attractiveness of imagination and love as one,[5] one sees through this bogus oneness soon enough and hates 'the very idea of it'. What now? Total avoidance of all virtual reality is practically impossible. However the solution is the one that works for us in relation to the entire popular domain, which is respect. What we respect cannot harm us. Ex-

---

[5] In other words, one is fatally reminded of that time originally when imagination was not separate from love (the way a lie reminds us of the truth).

tinction itself is at least a fact and for the one who espouses world-mystery and true world-knowledge all facts are at least respectable. Nonetheless those who court extinction deeply concern us.

*

Not that we are no longer aware of imagination as such, once we have become fortified by world-mysterious sacrament, or by the awe-inspiring onset of world without end, also called kingdom of god on earth. I do however want to limit myself, in this essay, to what we might call some of the commencement features of world, such as the mystery of it, which appears strongest, most prominent at the start, and to which we may respond with delight and in awe.

Only we should not imagine that we can cause world to happen, the way we strike a match which causes fire to appear, or even the way we throw a ball in the air and cause it to fall to earth. Such causes are mechanistically imagined. A great deal is always left out of consideration before we suppose we are justified in making such causal connections, which do depend on infertile imagination, at best accompanied by conditional love. All of our modern physics, after all, of which we are so proud because it so effectively (to our minds) dispenses with merciful good spirit, boils down to such infertile imagination in combination with conditional love.

Nonetheless, even as there is a way in which we can open ourselves to the good spiritual realm within, where eventually the pleasure of god-presence becomes habitual, so we may outwardly too, due to the good we do while informed ethically from within, invite in this way world-revelation and world-dispensation.

*

It takes a religious man, a man with a religious bent to his born nature, to understand world revelation. To the moral approach such revelation is a closed book. Morality implies ser-

35

vice; however world-revelation is also a matter of contact with our human nature. This is what is meant by fundamental faith. 'Religious', in turn implies 'faithful'.

To the extent that we are also spiritual beings, in addition to being moral and religious, world-mystery appeals to us as an extension of our human being. The initially sacramental character of true world-experience alleviates our trend to self-absorption, our tendency to individualism, by drawing our attention to spiritual community and therefore to the need for contact with our human nature, which contact always needs to be renewed whenever we do our work in the world. As we set examples of world-relation in the world, we cannot help but be affected by the world, by this consummate desire for ego, so that time and again we need to be cleansed of worldly affects, metaphorically the washing of feet[6] now that all else is clean.

*

When world-mystery is truly absorbed by us and when we have internalized the sacramental substance, we are fulfilled and have no further wishes. However at the same time there is brewing within us, like the sourdough in an as yet unbaked loaf, the next extension of world which we incorporate. The world is like the womb out of which world is daily being borne by human beings. In our own way we translate the world of space, time and causality into world of eternal reference and affinity. After all we too are a mystery to ourselves when first we act out of the fullness of our human being and interact with others who are set upon a similar course. Since we have the works of those who live in their works and lived in the past too, there is literally no limit to the extent of our effectiveness. It is only when we try to imagine world in terms of the world or conversely when we think of ourselves as not readily equipped with the wherewithal for an appreciation of life and world in

---

[6] Compare Gospel of John; 13:10-14.

unison, that we cling to outworn trials and temptations as though from them we might garner what we miss, while of our human nature we know nothing but its carnal dimension and meanwhile merciful good spirit remains enigmatic.

* * *

May 2016